Let's Go Together

Questions for Our Love,
A Bucket List For Our Dreams

Jeffrey Mason

Let's Go Together

ISBN: ISBN: 1986224708
ISBN-13: 978-1986224703

TO PAULA,
YOU CAME ALONG
AND CHANGED EVERYTHING

HOW TO USE THIS JOURNAL

Relationships are supposed to be hard work.

I understand if you disagree with that sentence. We've all been raised on books and movies that teach us how easy this all is: fate brings us together, romance takes over, and then it's happily ever after. Finding and getting each other is where the we are supposed to put in the work. Once you check the box you get to move straight to the white picket fence and the kids and the mini-van.

If you tell someone that you need to get home to work on your relationship, you will most likely get an "Oh, I'm sorry. You guys seem so happy.

It's normal and even admirable to work on our careers. We set time aside to work on our fitness. Our evenings are scheduled with must watch television and our weekends have required sports viewing, but we can't seem to find the time to sit down and talk. We expect feedback from our boss on how we're doing at work, but bristle and get uncomfortable if our partner shares with us something that is bothering him or her.

Most relationships follow the same path. In the beginning, we're excited and romantic and passionate. We can't get enough of each other, and we bend our schedules to be together. That eventually leads to a committed phase where we update our social media status, meet families, and often combine households,

Then life kicks in, and jobs and kids and responsibilities take over our lives, and we default to the idea that being together removes the need to spend time together. There you are, two separate people with individual histories and perspectives and needs, and for some reason, we think that all we need to do is commit to each other and that is that. Job done. Work completed.

My personal story and what I have seen in others has convinced me that the work is never supposed to stop. The crazier and busier life gets, the more time you need as a couple. This is supposed to be your base, the place that once upon a time made you smile and glow and quiver and dream.

What do I mean by work? It's compromising and learning and giving and forgiving and being honest and vulnerable. It's setting time aside every day to pause and be together. Sometimes that time is a half hour, and sometimes it is an entire afternoon, but the point is to be together and share and plan like you did before you "got each other."

There are fifty days of work within these pages. Each day has a place for you to write down and plan something you want to do together. This is your couple's bucket list. Scheme and dream and plan for the life you want and the things you want to experience together. Go big but make sure you can lay down a way to make it happen.

The second part of each day is a question meant to help you learn about yourself and each other. The idea is to be open and vulnerable and to listen to each other. Finding a way to express ourselves and our needs to the most important person in our world creates opportunities for growth and understanding and intimacy. It will prevent barriers, make it easier to talk, and help develop a habit of spending intentional time together.

BUCKET LIST

The first section of each day's work is where you plan one item from your couple's bucket list. It can be travel or a big purchase or an event or having children, but the idea is that this is something you both want to do together.

Goals give your life structure and purpose. Without them, you would move along with no direction and no motivation. Goals tell you where you want to go and they give you a framework for your actions and your priorities. Relationships needs aspirations in the same way you as an individual does. This will probably require some compromises, but part of being in a relationship means altering something you want to make it something both of you want.

Make goals that excite you and motivate you. Be specific and give them a deadline and create a plan to make it happen. If you want to travel to Europe, write,

> *"By the end of the year _____, we will have traveled to Rome and Paris. To make this happen, we will start saving $_____ each week just for this purpose. We will check in every month with each other to see how our saving is progressing and how motivated we are to do this together."*

This paragraph specifies what the goal is, it tells you when it will occur, it has the plan to make it happen, and it has a mechanism for regular status checks. Turning an idea or a dream into reality is a matter of attaching a date and a plan to it and then acting on it.

Dream-Plan-Act-Reality.

QUESTIONS

There are two purposes to the questions in this workbook. The first is to learn about each other, yourselves, and your relationship. Learning best occurs when you open your mind, you fully participate, and you listen.

The majority of the questions in this book are intended for each of you to talk about your perspective on a topic. There is no wrong or right. The idea is to learn how and why each of you feels and thinks. Trust is key and the best way to preserve it is to avoid judging or becoming personal.

The second purpose of each question is to create a habit of setting aside time each day to sit down with each other and talk openly and honestly. My personal experience is that the more you don't talk about something, the more likely it is you will eventually argue about it. Tucking our feelings and needs away creates festering, irritation, and resentment. If your partner is doing something that upsets or concerns you, pause and, with empathy, talk to them about it and work together to figure it out.

If you come across a question that causes either or both of you discomfort, sit down separately, and think about it. Dig deep and try to figure out the root of the emotions and feelings the question has created. Write this down. In a few days, come back to the question and talk openly about why you were uncomfortable. Help the other person understand how they can help you feel more secure.

Another tip is to allow silence. There will be times when you will find the other person pausing and needing to think about how they will answer. Don't make the mistake of thinking that this is a sign of avoiding the question. Give them time and let them find the words that they are comfortable using. Listen, and when they finish, thank them and ask, "Is there anything else?" The point is to always work together.

I'm excited for the two of you. I know that this will initially feel awkward and scary, but I promise that if you strive to learn from each other and work to make your dreams a reality, you will foster a relationship full of closeness and intimacy and love and strength.

"Though nobody can go back and make a new beginning...
Anyone can start over and make a new ending."
— Chico Xavier

1 We Will

By When?

What is our plan to make this happen?

What will accomplishing this do for our relationship?

"The world as we have created it is a process of our thinking. It cannot be changed without changing our thinking."— Albert Einstein

Date This Item Was Accomplished ________________

Favorite memory? ________________________________
____
____
____

What did we learn about each other? ______________
____
____
____

Our Question

Learning another person's life story provides an understanding of who they are. It helps give insight into their perspectives, their beliefs, their choices, and their priorities.

Tell each other your individual life stories. Take ten minutes, and include at least two life-changing moments, two achievements, and two failures. The key is to be open and vulnerable. Listen to each other and avoid interrupting or commenting. When they finish, show your gratitude and share what you learned and how it helps you understand them better.

"Take my hand and we'll make it…I swear."
– Jon Bon Jovi, Livin' On a Prayer

2 We Will

By When?

What is our plan to make this happen?

What will accomplishing this do for our relationship?

"The greatest thing you will ever learn is to just love and be loved in return."- Nat King Cole, Nature Boy

Date This Item Was Accomplished ________________

Favorite memory? ______________________________
____
____
____
____

What did we learn about each other? ____________
____
____
____
____

Our Question

It is often the small things that have the most significant impact. Tell each other the specific things they do and identify what best show their love and affection. Share the additional things they could do that would be an essential and meaningful display of their love and appreciation. What is the best way the other person can communicate their need for more affection or closeness?

"What's meant to be will always find a way."
- Trisha Yearwood

3 We Will

By When?

What is our plan to make this happen?

What will accomplishing this do for our relationship?

"I could stay with you forever and never realize the time."
—Bob Dylan

Date This Item Was Accomplished ________________

Favorite memory? ______________________________
____
____
____

What did we learn about each other? ____________
____
____

Our Question

It is understandable how the longer we are together, the less of a priority spending quality time together can become. Work and life can take over schedules, and we default into thinking that because we are together, we don't need to spend time together. Studies show the importance regular quality time as a couple plays in increasing happiness, intimacy, and relationship longevity. Do you have a scheduled time set aside for just the two of you?

Work together to plan a regular time to spend time together. Agree on the purpose of these times and commit to excluding technology.

"Always be a first rate version of yourself and not a second rate version of someone else." – Judy Garland

4 We Will

____
____
____
____

By When? ________________________________

____

What is our plan to make this happen?

____
____
____
____
____
____
____

What will accomplishing this do for our relationship?

____
____
____
____
____

"In order to be irreplaceacle, one must always be different."
– Coco Chanel

Date This Item Was Accomplished ____________

Favorite memory? ________________________

____

____

____

What did we learn about each other? __________

____

____

Our Question

Spending time together is essential, but so is spending time by ourselves. Being alone helps us to focus on our personal needs and passions. It helps us to recharge. Time apart can increase fondness, attraction, and intimacy. The amount of needed time alone varies from individual to individual, so work together to determine what is comfortable, practical, and effective.

Discuss with each other the best way to communicate their need for time by themselves. Include standard occurrences or moments that can create this need.

"He is the cheese to my macaroni."
– Diablo Cody, Juno

5 We Will

By When?

What is our plan to make this happen?

What will accomplishing this do for our relationship?

"one's not half of two; two are halves of one."
– E.E. Cummings

Date This Item Was Accomplished ________________

Favorite memory? ______________________________
____
____

What did we learn about each other? ____________
____
____

Our Question

Communication and intimacy can be blocked when we assume what the other person needs or when we are unclear in what we require. Miscommunications can lead to avoidable issues and misperceptions.

Sit down together and write how the other person communicates is working and is not working. Is there an approach that works best for you? Remember that we all have different needs and styles, and these issues aren't just one person's fault. Work together to find a way to add the questions "What can I do for you?" and "What do you need from me?" to your daily relationship and how you talk to each other.

"It may be unfair, but what happens in a few days, sometimes even a single day, can change the course of a whole lifetime.." – Khaled Hosseini, The Kite Runner

6 We Will

By When?

What is our plan to make this happen?

What will accomplishing this do for our relationship?

"We delight in the beauty of the butterfly, but rarely admit the changes it has gone through to achieve that beauty."
– Maya Angelou

Date This Item Was Accomplished ______________

Favorite memory? ______________________________
____
____
____

What did we learn about each other? ___________
____
____
____
____

Our Question

A habit is defined as a regular tendency that is hard to give up. We all have them, and while most are harmless, many can cause displeasure for the other person in our relationship.

Discuss any habits the other person has that bother or concern you. Avoid making the discussion personal. Work together to make any suggested changes and remember that breaking a habit or creating a new one takes patience and focus and empathy.

"if the relationship can't survive the long term, why on earth would it be worth my time and energy for the short term" – Nicholas Sparks, The Last Song

7 We Will

____

____

____

____

By When? ______________________

____

What is our plan to make this happen?

____

____

____

____

____

____

____

What will accomplishing this do for our relationship?

____

____

____

____

"Last night, I got up the courage to ask you if you regretted us. "There are things I miss," you said. "But if I didn't have you, I'd miss more."— David Levithan

Date This Item Was Accomplished ______________

Favorite memory? ______________________
____
____
____

What did we learn about each other? ___________
____
____
____
____

Our Question

Share with each other a time you had your heart broken. What did you learn from the experience and what helped you move on? Has this situation or one like it ever created issues or hesitancy in a later relationship? What is the best way for each of you to communicate when the past is impacting how the two of you interact? What can you do together when these situations arise and what can you do to prevent them?

"Every man I meet wants to protect me. I can't figure out what from"— Mae West

8 We Will

By When?

What is our plan to make this happen?

What will accomplishing this do for our relationship?

"The moment you doubt whether you can fly, you cease for ever to be able to do it." – J.M. Barrie, Peter Pan

Date This Item Was Accomplished ________________

Favorite memory? ________________________________

____

____

____

What did we learn about each other? ______________

____

____

____

____

Our Question

Talk about a time feeling insecure stopped you from doing something. Looking back, how would you handle the same situation if it occurred today? How can you help each other if similar feelings arise in the future?

Do either of you have any insecurities that are impacting your relationship? What can you do for each other to help mitigate these feelings?

"When you're at the end of your rope, tie a knot and hold on.."— Theodore Roosevelt

9 We Will

____
____
____
____

By When? ________________________________

____

What is our plan to make this happen?

____
____
____
____
____
____
____

What will accomplishing this do for our relationship?

____
____
____
____
____

"If you are going through hell, keep going."
— Winston Churchill

Date This Item Was Accomplished ________________

Favorite memory? ______________________________
____
____
____

What did we learn about each other? ____________
____
____
____
____
____

Our Question

Talk about a time when you had to overcome a significant challenge. What did you learn about yourself and others from the experience?

Is there a current situation you find challenging? What can the two of you do together to address the situation?

"It's not hard to make decisions when you know what your values are" — Roy Disney

10 We Will

____

____

____

____

By When? ______________________________

____

What is our plan to make this happen?

____

____

____

____

____

____

____

What will accomplishing this do for our relationship?

____

____

____

____

____

"Bear in mind that the measure of a man is the
things he cares about." — Marcus Aurel

Date This Item Was Accomplished ________

Favorite memory? ________________________________

____

____

____

What did we learn about each other? ____________

____

____

____

____

Our Question

Values are firmly held beliefs about yourself and the world and are vital in knowing who you are and who you want to be. Values help steer your life and provide purpose and motivation and make decisions easier.

Separately, write down your personal core values. Compare and discuss each other's list. Work together to define your relationship's core values. Discuss how your current relationship matches your list, and work together to make any changes.

Whenever you are about to find fault with someone, ask yourself...: What fault of mine most nearly resembles the one I am about to criticize?" — Marcus Aurelius, Meditations

11 We Will

By When?

What is our plan to make this happen?

What will accomplishing this do for our relationship?

"You never really understand a person until you consider things from his point of view... Until you climb inside of his skin and walk around in it" — Harper Lee

Date This Item Was Accomplished ______________

Favorite memory? ______________________________

____

____

____

What did we learn about each other? ____________

____

____

____

Our Question

Understanding our partner's daily routine allows us to anticipate his or her needs and sympathize with his or her perspectives.

Working separately, write out a detailed description of the other person's typical day. Be specific and include any positive and negative things he or she may experience. Then, without sharing what you have written, take turns describing your typical day and then compare what you have written. What did you learn from each other, and how has this helped you better understand them?

"Do one thing every day that scares you."
— Eleanor Roosevelt

12 We Will

By When?

What is our plan to make this happen?

What will accomplishing this do for our relationship?

"The secret to getting ahead is getting started."
— Mark Twain

Date This Item Was Accomplished ________________

Favorite memory? ________________________________

____

____

____

What did we learn about each other? ____________

____

____

____

____

Our Question

Take five minutes for each of you to separately describe your ideal life. Be specific and take time to think of as many details as you can of the life you want. Discuss what is similar and different in each of your descriptions and what you may find surprising. What did you learn about each other from what you wrote?

Pick one thing on both lists and construct a plan for the two of to work together you to achieve them.

"It is said that your life flashes before your eyes just before you die. That is true, it's called Life."
—Terry Pratchett, The Last Continent

13 We Will

____

____

____

____

By When? ________________________

____

What is our plan to make this happen?

____

____

____

____

____

____

____

What will accomplishing this do for our relationship?

____

____

____

____

____

"A life spent making mistakes is not only more honorable, but more useful than a life spent doing nothing."
— George Bernard Shaw

Date This Item Was Accomplished ________________

Favorite memory? ________________________________

____

____

____

What did we learn about each other? ______________

____

____

____

____

Our Question

While it is impossible to change things we regret in our lives, it is essential that we learn everything possible from these moments. How we feel about the past provides valuable clues on how we can make better choices.

Looking back on your life, what is something you would do differently? What can this experience teach you about a change you should make or what your priorities should be?

"When I started counting my blessings, my whole life turned around"— Willie Nelson

14 We Will

____

____

____

____

By When? ________________________________

____

What is our plan to make this happen?

____

____

____

____

____

____

____

What will accomplishing this do for our relationship?

____

____

____

____

____

"Let us be grateful to the people who make us happy; they are the charming gardeners who make our souls blossom."
— Marcel Proust

Date This Item Was Accomplished ______________

Favorite memory? ______________________________
____
____
____

What did we learn about each other? ____________
____
____
____
____

Our Question

List five things about yourself and five things about the other person that you are grateful for.

Joe	Myself
1. The life we have 2gether	1. My Health
2. our Partnership	2. my work ethic
3. our sense of humor	3. my friends
4. our travels	4. my Family
5. The time we get to spend at the Lakes	5. making a difference in Childrens life

6 Akryn

"A friend is someone who knows all about you and still loves you."— Elbert Hubbard

15 We Will

____

____

____

____

____

By When? ______________________________

____

What is our plan to make this happen?

____

____

____

____

____

____

____

What will accomplishing this do for our relationship?

____

____

____

____

____

"I would rather walk with a friend in the dark, than alone in the light." – Helen Keller

Date This Item Was Accomplished ______________

Favorite memory? ______________________________

____

____

____

____

What did we learn about each other? ____________

____

____

____

Our Question

Some of our most important relationships are our friendships. They teach us valuable lessons about ourselves and what we need from another person.

What do you value most in a friend? Do you get to spend enough time with your friends? Is there any resentment in your relationship over the issue of time spent with friends? Discuss what you can do together to ensure you can maintain your friendships while also being mindful of each other's feelings. Discuss and work through any resentments or concerns over outside friendships.

"For the two of us, home isn't a place. It is a person.
And we are finally home."
— Stephanie Perkins, Anna & the French Kiss

16 We Will

By When?

What is our plan to make this happen?

What will accomplishing this do for our relationship?

"Anyone can live in a house, but homes are created with patience, time and love."— Jane Green

Date This Item Was Accomplished ________________

Favorite memory? ______________________________

____

____

____

____

What did we learn about each other? ____________

____

____

____

____

Our Question

Our homes are more than just a place for our stuff and where we sleep. Whether it is a house or an apartment or a trailer or boat, our homes are more than just the place we live; this is the place we create memories, and we can be ourselves. Our homes should be comfortable and inspiring, and it should generate a sense of safety.

Talk with each other about what you like about your home. What are the things you would change? Is there a specific spot that you especially enjoy?

"You may say I'm a dreamer, but I'm not the only one."
— John Lennon

17 We Will

By When?

What is our plan to make this happen?

What will accomplishing this do for our relationship?

"There is only one thing that makes a dream impossible to achieve: the fear of failure."— Paulo Coelho, The Alchemist

Date This Item Was Accomplished ______________

Favorite memory? ______________________________

____

____

____

____

What did we learn about each other? ____________

____

____

____

____

Our Question

What dream have you given up because you decided it was unrealistic? What made you feel this way?

The trick to turning a dream into reality is to create a plan to achieve it, and a specific day it will be done. Adding a date to a dream turns it into a goal and adding a strategy to a goal is the first step to making it real. What are your individual dreams, and what are your dreams as a couple? Work together to create priorities, specific strategies, and deadlines for all of your dreams.

"There are years that ask questions and years that answer."
— Zora Neale Hurston, Their Eyes Were Watching God

18 We Will

By When?

What is our plan to make this happen?

What will accomplishing this do for our relationship?

"None of us really changes over time. We only become more fully what we are." — Anne Rice, The Vampire Lestat

Date This Item Was Accomplished ________________

Favorite memory? ______________________________

____

____

____

What did we learn about each other? ______________

____

____

____

____

Our Question

An inevitable condition of life is that things change, and we change. Whether we initiate it or it happens to us, change can be discomforting, especially if we are unable to come to terms with its impacts.

Talk with each other a current change in your life that concerns you. Why do you think you feel this way? Is there a change the two of you want to make in your relationship over the next twelve months. Work together to create a plan to help this happen.

"Never go to bed mad. Stay up and fight."
– Phyllis Diller

19 We Will

By When?

What is our plan to make this happen?

What will accomplishing this do for our relationship?

"The greatest remedy for anger is delay."
— Thomas Paine

Date This Item Was Accomplished ______________

Favorite memory? ______________________________
____
____
____
____

What did we learn about each other? ___________
____
____
____
____

Our Question

Anger is a normal human emotion, but it can create negative feelings in others if we are unable to control ourselves in these moments.

Individually, write how you feel you express your anger and how the other person shows theirs. Compare and discuss. Have there been instances when the other person's anger made you uncomfortable? Are there things either of you should avoid saying or doing in these moments? What can you do together to plan for and manage these moments?

"Do not go where the path may lead, go instead where there is no path and leave a trail."
— Ralph Waldo Emerson

20 We Will

By When?

What is our plan to make this happen?

What will accomplishing this do for our relationship?

"Why join the navy if you can be a pirate"
— Steve Jobs

Date This Item Was Accomplished ________________

Favorite memory? ______________________________
____
____
____
____

What did we learn about each other? ______________
____
____
____
____

Our Question

There are times in life when we have to make unpopular decisions. When our choices go against what everyone else expects or wants, the resulting rifts and regrets can linger. Whether these decisions are elected by us or forced upon us, the key is to focus on moving forward and concentrate on what we can control.

Talk with each other about a time when you made an unpopular decision. Was the result positive or negative? What did you learn about yourself and would you do it again?

"I don't want to die without any scars."
— Chuck Palahniuk, Fight Club

21 We Will

____
____
____
____

By When? ________________________________

____

What is our plan to make this happen?

____
____
____
____
____
____
____

What will accomplishing this do for our relationship?

____
____
____
____
____
____

"You only live once, but if you do it right,
once is enough" — Mae West

Date This Item Was Accomplished ________________

Favorite memory? ____________________________

____

____

____

What did we learn about each other? ___________

____

____

____

____

Our Question

Part of being human is a desire to leave our mark behind. For many, this can be through their careers or their art, while for others, it is through their children.

Talk about something significant each of you wants to achieve in your lifetime. What are you currently doing to make this happen, and what are you willing to do and risk? What are ways the two of you can work together to make this a reality?

"When you don't talk, there's a lot of stuff
that ends up not getting said."
— Catherine Gilbert Murdock, Dairy Queen

22 We Will

____

____

____

____

By When? ________________________________

____

What is our plan to make this happen?

____

____

____

____

____

____

What will accomplishing this do for our relationship?

____

____

____

____

____

____

"The strongest love is the love that can demonstrate its fragility." — Paulo Coelho

Date This Item Was Accomplished ______________

Favorite memory? ____________________________

____

____

____

____

What did we learn about each other? ___________

____

____

____

____

Our Question

It is common, even in the closest relationships, for there to be a hesitancy to discuss specific topics. These feelings can be rooted in fear or embarrassment or a past negative experience.

What is a topic that is uncomfortable for you to discuss with the other person? Why? Is there something they have expressed in the past that prevents you from doing so? What can you do together that would make it easier to discuss difficult topics?

"Remember, Hope is a good thing, maybe the best of things, and no good thing ever dies."— Stephen King

23 We Will

By When?

What is our plan to make this happen?

What will accomplishing this do for our relationship?

"My optimism wears heavy boots and is loud."
— Henry Rollins

Date This Item Was Accomplished ________________

Favorite memory? ________________________________
____
____
____
____

What did we learn about each other? ______________
____
____
____
____

Our Question

Life is full of challenges, some big and some small, and how we manage these situations can vary from person to person. Even the most optimistic person can face circumstances that make it difficult to remain hopeful.

Talk about a time when a situation made it difficult to be positive. How did this affect you? How do you think you would handle a similar situation today? Talk openly about how the other person should act in these moments and what you think you would need from them.

"It is not a lack of love, but a lack of friendship that makes an unhappy marriage"— Friedrich Nietzsche

24 We Will

____
____
____
____

By When? ______________________________
____

What is our plan to make this happen?

____
____
____
____
____
____
____

What will accomplishing this do for our relationship?

____
____
____
____
____

"True love is friendship set on fire."
— Molly E. Lee, Edge of Chaos

Date This Item Was Accomplished ________________

Favorite memory? ________________________________
____
____
____

What did we learn about each other? ______________
____
____
____

Our Question

An essential component of maintaining a fulfilling long-term love relationship is fostering and nurturing the friendship you have with each other. Making this the foundation of who you are as a couple is how longevity in romance and intimacy is maintained and you avoid a relationship fueled only by responsibilities.

A true friendship is based on mutual respect, openness, and companionship. Friends listen to each other and are there for each other. What is the state of your friendship? Work together to identify ways to make this part of your relationship stronger.

"If you want something new, you have to stop doing something old."— Peter F. Drucker

25 We Will

____

____

____

____

By When? ________________________

____

What is our plan to make this happen?

____

____

____

____

____

____

____

What will accomplishing this do for our relationship?

____

____

____

____

____

____

"We are what we repeatedly do. Excellence, then, is not an act, but a habit." — William Durant

Date This Item Was Accomplished ______________

Favorite memory? ______________________________

____

____

____

What did we learn about each other? ____________

____

____

____

Our Question

Significant changes in life typically occur by making small incremental changes to the routines you keep and the choices you make. Over time, these changes accumulate to create noticeable and impactful movements in who we are, what we're about, and what kind of lives we lead.

What is one small thing you can start doing today that would begin moving life in the direction you want? Discuss potential ideas with each other and work together to create a plan for the two of you to start moving forward and hold each other accountable.

"because being with you makes perfect sense"
– Tim McGraw

26 We Will

____
____
____
____

By When? ________________________

____

What is our plan to make this happen?

____
____
____
____
____
____
____

What will accomplishing this do for our relationship?

____
____
____
____
____
____

"I fell in love the way you fall asleep: slowly, and then all at once" —John Green, The Fault in Our Stars

Date This Item Was Accomplished ________________

Favorite memory? ________________________________
____
____
____

What did we learn about each other? ____________
____
____
____
____
____

Our Question

The memories we have of each other can be the glue and the language of our relationships. They are also an excellent way to measure the state of how strong a couple is. The more distant your memories are, the more likely the two of you aren't nurturing your romance and your friendship.

Talk about some favorite memories of the two of you together. Be open and discuss the feelings they create. How distant are these memories, and have they changed over time? What can the two of you do to create opportunities for new memories?

"I wonder how many people don't get the one they want,
but end up with the one they're supposed to be with"
– Fannie Flagg, Fried Green Tomatoes

27 We Will

____

____

____

____

By When? ______________________________

____

What is our plan to make this happen?

____

____

____

____

____

____

____

What will accomplishing this do for our relationship?

____

____

____

____

____

"I may not have gone where I intended to go, but I think I have ended up where I needed to be" — Douglas Adams

Date This Item Was Accomplished ________________

Favorite memory? ________________________________

____

____

____

What did we learn about each other? ______________

____

____

____

____

____

Our Question

Most of us can think back to a single event or decision that changed the course of our lives or changed who we are. Talk about a moment from your past that changed the direction of your life.

Looking back, what role do you think impacts how you act and the choices you make today? In what positive and negative ways does it affect your current relationship? What can the two of you do together to mitigate any harm this moment may be causing for the two of you?

"The individual who says it is not possible should move out of the way of those doing it." — Tricia Cunningham

28 We Will

____
____
____
____

By When? ______________________________
____

What is our plan to make this happen?

____
____
____
____
____
____
____

What will accomplishing this do for our relationship?

____
____
____
____
____

"The only person you are destined to become is the person you decide to be." — Ralph Waldo Emerson

Date This Item Was Accomplished ________________

Favorite memory? ________________________________

____

____

____

What did we learn about each other? ______________

____

____

____

Our Question

Taking turns after listing each one, name three personal goals each of you have. Work together to put them in the order to be accomplished. Discuss ways you can achieve your highest ranked goals and write out your plans for achieving them. Include the changes and sacrifices you are going to make.

Set aside time each week for the two of you to provide progress updates, work on any issues, give support, and provide accountability. If you have children, consider adding them to your conversations to expose them to the concepts of goal setting and ways to accomplish them.

"My favorite thing is to go where I've never been"
— Diane Arbus

29 We Will

____
____
____
____

By When? ____________________________

____

What is our plan to make this happen?

____
____
____
____
____
____
____

What will accomplishing this do for our relationship?

____
____
____
____
____
____

"As soon as I saw you, I knew an adventure was going to happen"— Winnie the Pooh

Date This Item Was Accomplished ______________

Favorite memory? ______________________________

____

____

____

____

What did we learn about each other? ____________

____

____

____

____

____

Our Question

Travel is a great way to discover things about yourself and each other and who you are as a couple. Spending extended amounts of time in new environments and unique places creates self-confidence and inspires us to try new things.

What is a place each of you has always wanted to visit but never have? Make traveling to each destination a relationship goal. Create a plan to make it each one a reality.

"Rock bottom became the solid foundation on which I rebuilt my life" — J.K. Rowling

30 We Will

By When?

What is our plan to make this happen?

What will accomplishing this do for our relationship?

"You are not a failure until you start blaming others for your mistakes"— John Wooden

Date This Item Was Accomplished ________________

Favorite memory? ______________________________

____

____

____

____

What did we learn about each other? _____________

____

____

____

____

Our Question

Thomas Edison is credited with saying that he never failed and instead found 10,000 ways that didn't work. To Edison, failure was just part of the process of finding answers. Failure hurts, and it can lead to feelings of embarrassment, but it is also the key to growing as an individual. The key is to be accountable for your role in the failure, learn its lessons, and make any necessary changes.

Take turns talking about a failure from the past. What were the circumstances that created the situation? Specifically, talk about what you learned and how you moved forward.

"If you fell down yesterday, stand up today"— H.G. Wells

31 We Will

By When?

What is our plan to make this happen?

What will accomplishing this do for our relationship?

"He who limps is still walking"— Stanisław Jerzy Lec

Date This Item Was Accomplished _______________

Favorite memory? ______________________________

____

____

____

What did we learn about each other? _____________

____

____

____

____

Our Question

The ability to reframe a negative situation into a neutral or positive one is a valuable skill to develop. Life is full of moments that go against what we want or what we need, and it is critical that we be able to move forward. Possible tactics for dealing with these situations include trying to find the "silver lining," turning it into a personal challenge, looking for the lessons to be learned, and getting help from our support network.

Talk about a negative event from your past that you were able to make positive. What did you do to take control of this moment, and what did you learn about yourself and others who were involved?

"If you need something from somebody always give that person a way to hand it to you."— Sue Monk Kidd, The Secret Life of Bees

32 We Will

By When?

What is our plan to make this happen?

What will accomplishing this do for our relationship?

"Tact is the knack of making a point without making an enemy."— Isaac Newton

Date This Item Was Accomplished ________________

Favorite memory? ________________________________

____

____

____

What did we learn about each other? ____________

____

____

____

____

Our Question

Disagreements are a regular part of every relationship. The key is to be able to express your feelings while maintaining respect for the other person and their views.

Take a half-hour and work together to create a Disagreement Contract. Agree on a set of ground rules on how each of you will conduct yourself in these situations. Examples include avoiding anger, taking turns when talking, listening instead of interrupting, avoiding judgment or getting personal or negative. Make reaching an agreement, instead of being right, a priority.

"You can't wait for inspiration. You have to go after it with a club." — Jack London

33 We Will

____

____

____

____

By When? ________________________________

____

What is our plan to make this happen?

____

____

____

____

____

____

____

What will accomplishing this do for our relationship?

____

____

____

____

____

____

"Some people come in our life as blessings. Some come in your life as lessons."— Mother Teresa

Date This Item Was Accomplished ______________

Favorite memory? ____________________________

____

____

____

____

What did we learn about each other? ___________

____

____

____

____

____

Our Question

Many of us can trace our path in life back to a teacher, a librarian, or a coach. Educators and coaches can have a massive influence on our desire to learn, how we view the world, and how we see ourselves.

Tell each other about a teacher or a coach who had a significant influence on you growing up. What did they do to leave such a strong impression? How does your current life reflect their legacy? If you can still contact them, reach out to them to let them know how grateful you are for their impact.

"It's hard to beat a person who never gives up." – Babe Ruth

34 We Will

By When?

What is our plan to make this happen?

What will accomplishing this do for our relationship?

"There are no shortcuts to any place worth going.."
— Beverly Sills

Date This Item Was Accomplished ______________

Favorite memory? ______________________________

____

____

What did we learn about each other? ____________

____

____

Our Question

The strength of your relationship can be measured, and improved, by focusing on a few components of how you interact. Take a half hour and rank each other on a scale of one to five, without using the three, in the following areas:

- How well does your partner show their appreciation and affection for you?
- How effective of a communicator is the other person?
- Do the two of you share the same values?
- How would you rate your intimacy?
- Do they support you?

Discuss how you ranked each other and put together a plan to work on any needed improvements.

"Sometimes the questions are complicated and the answers are simple."— Dr. Seuss

35 We Will

____

____

____

____

By When? ________________________________

____

What is our plan to make this happen?

____

____

____

____

____

____

____

What will accomplishing this do for our relationship?

____

____

____

____

____

____

"What is wanted is not the will to believe, but the will to find out, which is the exact opposite."— Bertrand Russell

Date This Item Was Accomplished ______________

Favorite memory? ____________________________

____

____

____

____

What did we learn about each other? ___________

____

____

____

____

Our Question

A healthy relationship is one where each person is both a teacher and a student. Each of us has our own life story and experiences, and our individual strengths and weaknesses. This influences how we act, the choices we make, and how we love.

Discuss the specific things you have learned from each other. Talk about things you see in the other person that you admire and want to emulate. Are there things each of you can do or avoid doing to help the other person?

"True forgiveness is when you can say, "Thank you for that experience." — Oprah Winfrey

36 We Will

By When?

What is our plan to make this happen?

What will accomplishing this do for our relationship?

"You only have to forgive once. To resent, you have to do it all day, every day" — M.L. Stedman

Date This Item Was Accomplished ________________

Favorite memory? ________________________________

____

____

____

What did we learn about each other? ______________

____

____

____

Our Question

Research on the subject of forgiveness proves it to be a hugely impactful part of a relationship. A couple is two imperfect humans working in the space of vulnerability, creating an environment ripe for disappointment and heartache. Forgiveness is necessary for both individuals to endure these times and preserve the relationship's trust and intimacy.

How does each of you define forgiveness? Do you believe you have the capacity to forgive someone unconditionally? Are their specific things you would have a difficult time forgiving? Talk about a time you used forgiveness to free yourself and move on.

"So, I love you because the entire universe conspired to help me find you." — Paulo Coelho, The Alchemist

37 We Will

By When? ____________________

What is our plan to make this happen?

What will accomplishing this do for our relationship?

"But most of all I'm afraid of walking out that door and never feeling again for my whole life the way I feel when I'm with you"— Baby, Dirty Dancing

Date This Item Was Accomplished ______________

Favorite memory? ______________________________
____
____
____

What did we learn about each other? ____________
____
____
____
____

Our Question

Studies suggest that the way to obtain a more committed relationship is to focus on three factors:

- Compatibility: how does each person match with the other's needs?
- Satisfaction: how much pleasure and value does each one of you get from each other?
- Investment: how much do each of you contribute to and feel invested in the relationship.

Discuss together where you think you rank as a couple on these three factors. What can you do to make any desired improvments?

"Life isn't about finding yourself. Life is about creating yourself."— George Bernard Shaw

38 We Will

By When?

What is our plan to make this happen?

What will accomplishing this do for our relationship?

"Everything you can imagine is real"
– Pablo Picasso

Date This Item Was Accomplished ____________________

Favorite memory? ______________________________________

____

____

____

____

What did we learn about each other? ______________

____

____

____

____

____

____

Our Question

Spend at least five minutes describing for the other person what a perfect day would be like from beginning to end. Talk about the specific reasons that would make it such an ideal day. How does it compare to your typical day? Identify at least one thing in each other's story that you could add to your daily routine.

"Give out what you most want to come back."
— Robin S. Sharma

39 We Will

By When?

What is our plan to make this happen?

What will accomplishing this do for our relationship?

"Be the change that you wish to see in the world."
— Mahatma Gandhi

Date This Item Was Accomplished ________________

Favorite memory? ________________________________

____

____

____

____

____

What did we learn about each other? ______________

____

____

____

____

____

____

Our Question

Many of us feel drawn to impacting our communities and the world. Some of this desire results in participating in smaller acts such as volunteering or donations. Others decide to use their careers to work on an issue or a cause.

Is it important to you to make a change in the world? If you could pick anything, what would your focus be? Are there things you could start doing today to achieve this mission?

"Never love anyone who treats you like you're ordinary.."
— Oscar Wilde

40 We Will

By When?

What is our plan to make this happen?

What will accomplishing this do for our relationship?

"When I count my blessings, I find you in every one."
— Richelle E. Goodrich, Slaying Dragons

Date This Item Was Accomplished ________________

Favorite memory? ______________________________

____

____

____

____

____

What did we learn about each other? ____________

____

____

____

____

____

____

Our Question

What are three things I can do to better to show you how important you are to me?

1. ____
2. ____
3. ____

1. ____
2. ____
3. ____

"Aerodynamically, the bumble bee shouldn't be able to fly, but the bumble bee doesn't know it so it goes on flying anyway."— Mary Kay Ash

41 We Will

By When?

What is our plan to make this happen?

What will accomplishing this do for our relationship?

"The only way of discovering the limits of the possible is to venture a little way past them into the impossible"
— Arthur C. Clarke

Date This Item Was Accomplished ________________

Favorite memory? ________________________________

____

What did we learn about each other? ______________

____

____

Our Question

By definition, our "comfort zone" is the personal space where behaviors are made routine and systemized. The result is that these activities become stress- and anxiety-free, but staying within this zone can result in complacency in life. You can become risk adverse and unpracticed at dealing with significant events or challenges. Pushing ourselves outside our comfort zones can reveal capabilities we didn't know existed.

Is it hard going outside your comfort zone? If yes, try starting with small things such as mixing up your morning routine or wearing something you typically wouldn't. Talk about a time you went outside your comfort zone and what you learned about yourself.

"Appreciate the moment of a first kiss; it may be the last time you own your heart" — Robert M. Drake

42 We Will

____

____

____

____

By When? ______________________________

____

What is our plan to make this happen?

____

____

____

____

____

____

____

What will accomplishing this do for our relationship?

____

____

____

____

____

____

"I don't ask you to love me always like this, but I ask you to remember. Somewhere inside of me there will always be the person I am tonight" — F. Scott Fitzgerald

Date This Item Was Accomplished _______________

Favorite memory? _______________________________
____
____
____

What did we learn about each other? _____________
____
____
____
____
____
____
____

Our Question

Taking turns, talk about what you were thinking the first time you met each other. What were your first impressions of each other? Be descriptive and be open. What first impressions have lasted, and which ones have changed? What feelings and activities do you miss about the earliest days of your relationship? Work together to find ways to add back into your relationship.

"Death ends a life, not a relationship."
– Mitch Albom, Tuesdays with Morrie

43 We Will

____

____

____

____

By When? ______________________________

____

What is our plan to make this happen?

____

____

____

____

____

____

____

What will accomplishing this do for our relationship?

____

____

____

____

____

____

"It's better to burn out than to fade away."
— Neil Young

Date This Item Was Accomplished ________________

Favorite memory? ________________________________
____
____
____

What did we learn about each other? ______________
____
____
____

Our Question

Talking about the end of life can be hard, but avoiding it can lead to unfortunate consequences. We all deserve the dignity and empowerment of having our wishes followed at the end of life, but the challenge is our loved ones may react differently in these moments. Decisions can be influenced by grief or their own beliefs, with a negative impact on your family's lives for an extended period.

What are your wishes for the end of your life? What if you are incapacitated and unable to make health care decisions? Do each of you have a legal medical directive and a will to ensure your personal wishes are understood and followed?

"I would always rather be happy than dignified."
— Charlotte Brontë, Jane Eyre

44 We Will

By When?

What is our plan to make this happen?

What will accomplishing this do for our relationship?

"The problem with people is they forget that most of the time it's the small things that count."
— Jennifer Niven, All the Bright Places

Date This Item Was Accomplished _______________

Favorite memory? ______________________________
____
____
____

What did we learn about each other? ___________
____
____
____

Our Question

Happiness is important. It plays a role in our health and our relationships and our professional life. When we are happy, we tend to excel and be more involved, and our happiness can spread to what we do and those around us.

Do you know what makes you happy, and how do you define happiness? Without becoming personal or negative, talk about how your relationship adds to your ability to be happy and how it can interfere. How can you help each other when outside factors harm your satisfaction and joy? What changes can the two of you begin today that would assist both of you with your levels of happiness?

"Don't die without embracing the daring adventure your life was meant to be." — Steve Pavlina

45 We Will

By When? ______________________

What is our plan to make this happen?

What will accomplishing this do for our relationship?

"The biggest adventure you can take is to live the life of your dreams." — Oprah Winfrey

Date This Item Was Accomplished _______________

Favorite memory? ______________________________

____

____

____

What did we learn about each other? ____________

____

____

____

____

____

Our Question

Sometimes it's all about taking the dare. Making a risky choice can be scary, but it can also wake us from our monotony and teach us what we are capable of doing. You go from thinking you know what your limits are to seeing yourself and the world in a whole new way. Taking risk helps us grow, and it is often a necessary part of having the life we want for ourselves and our loved ones.

Tell each other about the most daring thing you have ever done. What did you learn about yourself from the experience?

"With the new day comes new strength and new thoughts."
– Eleanor Roosevelt

46 We Will

By When?

What is our plan to make this happen?

What will accomplishing this do for our relationship?

"A year from now you may wish you had started today"
— Karen Lamb

Date This Item Was Accomplished ______________
Favorite memory? ____________________________

____

____

____

____

____

____

____

What did we learn about each other? ____________

____

____

____

____

____

____

Our Question

Pick a goal that is achievable in a month or less for the two of you to work on together. Sit down and create a plan to accomplish the goal and set a due date and a reward for the two of you if it is completed.

"Be yourself; everyone else is already taken."— Oscar Wilde

47 We Will

By When?

What is our plan to make this happen?

What will accomplishing this do for our relationship?

"It's hard to be a diamond in a rhinestone world"
— Dolly Parton

Date This Item Was Accomplished ______________
Favorite memory? ___________________________

____

____

____

____

____

What did we learn about each other? ___________

____

____

____

Our Question

Humans have an innate need to belong to a group, but a downside to the desire to "fit in" is that it can alter the choices we make. Focusing on the opinions of can impact what we think and what we do to the point where they make who we are and our happiness secondary.

On a scale of one to five, without using the number three, rank how much you feel the other person lets outside opinions impact their choices. Talk about a decision you made in the past that you believe was profoundly influenced by the others. What would have been the result if you had been more independent in your decision?

"Too many people spend money they haven't earned, to buy things they don't want, to impress people that they don't like"— Will Rogers

48 We Will

____

____

____

____

By When? ________________________________

____

What is our plan to make this happen?

____

____

____

____

____

____

____

What will accomplishing this do for our relationship?

____

____

____

____

____

"If you want to know what God thinks of money, just look at the people he gave it to."— Dorothy Parker

Date This Item Was Accomplished ______________

Favorite memory? ____________________________

____

____

What did we learn about each other? ___________

____

____

Our Question

For many couples, money can be the source of many disagreements. These conversations can be emotional due to their connection with feelings of control and respect, and that is why it is essential for every couple to define together how they will have these talks.

When discussing money, focus on creating a space of trust and empathy. Avoid having to be right and instead work to listen to each other and find ways to agree and compromise. Together create a plan to eliminate debt and agree on a budget that provides both discipline and empowerment. Create one, five, and twenty year financial goals and evaluate how your current spending habits fit. Turn money check-ins into a regular discussion.

"Whatever our souls are made of, his and mine are the same." — Emily Bronte, Wuthering Heights

49 We Will

By When?

What is our plan to make this happen?

What will accomplishing this do for our relationship?

"Every breath that is in your lungs is a tiny little gift to me."
— The White Stripes, Dead Leave & The Dirty Ground

Date This Item Was Accomplished ________________

Favorite memory? ______________________________

____

____

____

____

____

____

What did we learn about each other? ____________

____

____

____

____

____

Our Question

Taking turns between each one, list five things about your partner that makes them unique and vital to your life. Be open and expressive and try to name things that only you would know.

Liv	Joe
1. Weirdness	1. smart very smart
2. Caring	2. weird in a great way/ goofy
3. Fun to laugh with/at	3. The way he loves to eat candy
4. Similar interests	4. His surprises
5. Annoying in a good way	5. How he's never serious and when he is its funny

"A friend is someone who knows all about you and still loves you." – Elbert Hubbard

50 We Will

By When?

What is our plan to make this happen?

What will accomplishing this do for our relationship?

"Any fool can know. The point is to understand."
– Albert Einstein

Date This Item Was Accomplished ________________

Favorite memory? ______________________________

____

____

____

____

What did we learn about each other? _____________

____

____

____

Our Question

The most direct path to accomplishing your goals is one that includes consistent formal opportunities to measure progress, evaluate strategies, and provide accountability.

Sit down and write a list of what you learned about yourself, each other, and your relationship over the past 90 days. Work together to create a list of things that are working on individually and those you are working on together. Come back to the list every 30 days to determine progress and to celebrate things you complete.

10 Reasons Couples Should Talk

1. It keeps them connected.
2. It helps them understand each other.
3. They learn about each other.
4. It prevents misperceptions and misunderstandings.
5. It preserves and enhances intimacy.
6. It helps the house run smoother.
7. It gives both people a place of comfort and safety.
8. It preserves the commitment.
9. It ensures they are on the same page on important topics such as money or children or goals.
10. It will help each of you grow as individuals.

10 Things Couples Should Talk About

1. Their individual and couple goals.
2. Things that upset or bother either of them.
3. What the other person does that you are grateful for.
4. Money.
5. Family.
6. Their needs and their wants.
7. Their feelings.
8. Their fears.
9. Their victories.
10. Their memories.

10 Ways To Talk About Money

1. Make talking about money a common topic. This prevents some of the anxiety and emotion this topic can create.
2. Avoid judging each other or the two of you as couple. Money is something you manage as opposed to use to create associated issues.
3. Take classes together on topics such as budgeting, retirement planning, credit scores, and paying off debts.
4. Never talk about money when either person is emotional.
5. Always work together to find the middle ground.
6. Consider using the services of a financial counselor.
7. Work together to create long and short term financial goals.
8. Agree on an "up to" per transaction/per week/month spending amount that both individuals would agree to.
9. Designate a person to pay the bills but have both parties participate.
10. Both individuals should have a separate credit card to maintain an individual credit record.

10 Topics That Can Be Tricky

1. Past relationships. Before starting ask yourself why you want/need to discuss your partner's relationship history. Make sure your level of communication promotes vulnerability and acceptance. Avoid judgement because we all have our history.
2. Sexual history. See #1.
3. Money conversations. Make sure you are prepared to discuss this topic together and make ensure you can avoid judgement.
4. Bringing up a past lie. This can be about a big or a small thing, but in both cases, never bring it up when emotional.
5. Anything negative about their family.
6. Anything negative about their friends.
7. Any sentence that begins with or is motivated by the phrase, "I am disappointed in you."
8. How to raise children. You should both agree but work together with patience and empathy to find your "house rules."
9. Anything motivated by a lack of trust.
10. Never insult each other or anything each other cares about. This is the moment you both agree to walk away and calm down and talk when the goal of finding compromise can be met.

OUR BUCKET LIST

1. ____________________
2. ____________________
3. ____________________
4. ____________________
5. ____________________
6. ____________________
7. ____________________
8. ____________________
9. ____________________
10. ____________________
11. ____________________
12. ____________________
13. ____________________
14. ____________________
15. ____________________
16. ____________________
17. ____________________
18. ____________________

OUR BUCKET LIST

19.____

20.____

21.____

22.____

23.____

24.____

25.____

26.____

27.____

28.____

29.____

30.____

31.____

32.____

33.____

34.____

35.____

36.____

OUR BUCKET LIST

37.______________________________

38.______________________________

39.______________________________

40.______________________________

41.______________________________

42.______________________________

43.______________________________

44.______________________________

45.______________________________

46.______________________________

47.______________________________

48.______________________________

49.______________________________

50.______________________________

51.______________________________

52.______________________________

53.______________________________

54.______________________________

OUR BUCKET LIST

55.______________________________

56.______________________________

57.______________________________

58.______________________________

59.______________________________

60.______________________________

61.______________________________

62.______________________________

63.______________________________

64.______________________________

65.______________________________

66.______________________________

67.______________________________

68.______________________________

69.______________________________

OUR BUCKET LIST

70.____

71.____

72.____

73.____

74.____

75.____

76.____

77.____

78.____

79.____

80.____

81.____

82.____

83.____

84.____

OUR BUCKET LIST

85.______________________________________

86.______________________________________

87.______________________________________

88.______________________________________

89.______________________________________

90.______________________________________

91.______________________________________

92.______________________________________

93.______________________________________

94.______________________________________

95.______________________________________

96.______________________________________

97.______________________________________

98.______________________________________

99.______________________________________

100. ____________________________________

My First Memory of You

My First Memory of You

My First Memory of You

My First Memory of You

Things You Do That Make Me Happy

1. ______________________________
2. ______________________________
3. ______________________________
4. ______________________________
5. ______________________________
6. ______________________________
7. ______________________________
8. ______________________________
9. ______________________________
10. ______________________________
11. ______________________________
12. ______________________________
13. ______________________________
14. ______________________________
15. ______________________________

Things You Do That Make Me Happy

1. ______________________________
2. ______________________________
3. ______________________________
4. ______________________________
5. ______________________________
6. ______________________________
7. ______________________________
8. ______________________________
9. ______________________________
10. ______________________________
11. ______________________________
12. ______________________________
13. ______________________________
14. ______________________________
15. ______________________________

More Questions to Ask Each Other

1. Who is the person you most admire?
2. What are your three wishes?
3. What is the weirdest dream you can remember?
4. What is your favorite childhood memory?
5. What is my favorite movie?
6. What is my favorite thing to eat?
7. How do you describe me to other people?
8. What is something I am scared of?
9. Do you remember the first words I said to you?
10. What do you remember our first kiss?
11. When did you first know that you loved me?
12. What is something I do that makes you feel loved.
13. If you were to give me a nickname, what would it be?
14. What movie reminds you of us?
15. What is your favorite song?
16. What is your favorite high school memory?
17. What is your most embarrassing high school memory?
18. Do you ever imagine yourself as a grandparent?
19. What would you want your last meal on Earth to be?
20. What three famous people would you want to invite for dinner?

More Questions to Ask Each Other

21. What is your dream job?
22. Do you have a favorite book?
23. Who was your favorite teacher growing up?
24. What is one thing you are great at?
25. What personal achievement are you most proud of?
26. Where do you want to be living in 10 years?
27. What would you buy if you had an extra $100 to spend on yourself?
28. What would you buy if you had an extra $,1000 to spend on yourself?
29. What is your most favorite vacation ever?
30. Who was your first crush?
31. What superpower would you pick for yourself?
32. What was your most favorite childhood pet ?
33. What is the one housekeeping task you would like to never have to do again?
34. What is your partner's favorite curse word?
35. What is my most annoying habit?
36. Who was your childhood best friend?
37. What was your hardest subject in school?
38. What five songs would be on your road trip playlist?
39. What is my shoe size?
40. What would be your perfect romantic weekend?

80 Fun Couple Activities

1. A fire in the backyard firepit for just the two of you.
2. Rent a convertible and go on a Sunday drive.
3. Watch the first movie you ever saw together.
4. Go on a picnic.
5. Mini-golf
6. See a movie at a local drive-in.
7. Go see a local play.
8. Take a ballroom dance class.
9. Be tourists in your own city.
10. Volunteer together for a cause you both care about.
11. Go for a hike
12. Hold a mini movie festival with both of each of your most favorite movies.
13. Visit a farmer's market and cook a meal together.
14. Paint a room.
15. Check out a local flea market.
16. Go to antique shopping.
17. Bowling. Sober or not.
18. Have a game night with yourself or friends.
19. Take a pottery or a painting class together.
20. Rent an ARBNB in a part of town you both love.

80 Fun Couple Activities

21. Go dancing.
22. Pitch a tent in the backyard and sleep outside.
23. Go wine tasting.
24. Wash the car together by hand.
25. Have a home cocktail night where you listen to jazz and mix drinks.
26. Find an fun activity on GroupOn.
27. Check out a local high school theater production.
28. Make a sheet tent in the living room and sleep in it.
29. Buy and use a couple hammock for the backyard.
30. Workout together.
31. Check out a local dive bar.
32. Play video games at a local arcade.
33. Go to a local coffee spot together and have a distraction free conversation.
34. Play cards.
35. Go to a local sporting event.
36. Look through old photos together.
37. Brunch!
38. Bake together.
39. Go see a show at a local comedy club.
40. Plan a mystery date where the other person has to find you based on a series of clues.

80 Fun Couple Activities

41. Go on a double date.
42. Find a local spot to watch the sunset.
43. Go to an amusement park without the kids.
44. Take a cooking class together.
45. Use Door Dash or PostMates to order each other a mystery dinner that you eat at the same time.
46. Go on a local tour.
47. Have a dinner of just finger food.
48. Check out the local zoo.
49. Play strip poker
50. Plant a garden together.
51. Plan your dream couple road trip.
52. Take an improv class together.
53. Learn how to brew beer.
54. Go to a local art exhibit.
55. Give each other a massage.
56. Dress up and go out for an amazing dinner.
57. Binge watch a television series from the past.
58. Have fondue at home.
59. Go for a bike ride.
60. Ice skating

80 Fun Couple Activities

61. Roller skating
62. Go to a record store and dig through albums.
63. Pick berries.
64. Have a spa day together.
65. Surprise your partner with a mystery weekend get-away.
66. Learn a language together.
67. Go shopping and have each other try on clothes you pick.
68. Check out an "Open Mike" night at a local bar.
69. Watch a scary movie together.
70. Have a no technology weekend.
71. Crash a wedding together.
72. Put together a puzzle.
73. Play a game from your childhood like twister or Operation or Life.
74. Have a Sunday in bed.
75. Plant flowers in your yard.
76. Make banana splits at home.
77. Play laser tag.
78. Go to a Karaoke bar together.
79. Go hit balls at a local driving range.
80. Turn your bedroom into a fancy hotel with items such as robes, towels, a mini bar, and a "Do Not Disturb" sign.

Quotes to Couple By

“I'm oxygen and he's dying to breathe.”
— Tahereh Mafi, Shatter Me

"Maybe you don’t need the whole world to love you, you know, maybe you just need one person."
— Kermit the Frog

"Being deeply loved by someone gives you strength, while loving someone deeply gives you courage."
— Laozi

"A heart that loves is always young."
— Greek Proverb

“I'm selfish, impatient and a little insecure. I make mistakes, I am out of control and at times hard to handle. But if you can't handle me at my worst, then you sure as hell don't deserve me at my best.”
— Marilyn Monroe

“You know you're in love when you can't fall asleep because reality is finally better than your dreams.”
— Dr. Seuss

"To love someone is nothing, to be loved by someone is something, to love someone who loves you is everything" — Bill Russell

Quotes to Couple By

"Never love anyone who treats you like you're ordinary." — Oscar Wilde

"We loved with a love that was more than love." — Edgar Allan Poe

"True love begins when nothing is looked for in return." — Antoine de Saint-Exupery

"He's more myself than I am. Whatever our souls are made of, his and mine are the same." — Emily Brontë, Wuthering Heights

"When love is not madness it is not love." — Pedro Calderón de la Barca

"If she's amazing, she won't be easy. If she's easy, she won't be amazing. If she's worth it, you won't give up. If you give up, you're not worthy. ... Truth is, everybody is going to hurt you; you just gotta find the ones worth suffering for." — Bob Marley

"They say a person needs just three things to be truly happy in this world: someone to love, something to do, and something to hope for." — Tom Bodett

Quotes to Couple By

I believe that two people are connected at the heart, and it doesn't matter what you do, or who you are or where you live; there are no boundaries or barriers if two people are destined to be together.
— Julia Roberts

"True love is rare, and it's the only thing that gives life real meaning."
— Nicholas Sparks, Message in a Bottle

"Life is short. Kiss slowly, laugh insanely, love truly and forgive quickly" — Paulo Coelho

"Man may have discovered fire, but women discovered how to play with it."
— Candace Bushnell, Sex and the City

"Never close your lips to those whom you have already opened your heart." — Charles Dickens

"Anyone can love a rose, but it takes a lot to love a leaf." — Tom Flynn

"And, in the end
The love you take
is equal to the love you make."
— Paul McCartney

Quotes to Couple By

"We're all a little weird. And life is a little weird. And when we find someone whose weirdness is compatible with ours, we join up with them and fall into mutually satisfying weirdness—and call it love—true love." — Robert Fulghum, True Love

"The Very first moment I beheld him, my heart was irrevocably gone."
— Jane Austen, Love and Friendship

"Beauty is not in the face; beauty is a light in the heart." — Khalil Gibran

"Love is a fire. But whether it is going to warm your hearth or burn down your house, you can never tell." — Joan Crawford

"Romance is the glamour which turns the dust of everyday life into a golden haze. " — Elinor Glyn

"Nothing is impossible, the word itself says 'I'm possible'!" — Audrey Hepburn

"In all the world, there is no heart for me like yours. In all the world, there is no love for you like mine."
— Maya Angelou

Quotes to Couple By

"Sometimes people put up walls, not to keep others out, but to see who cares enough to break them down." — Banana Yoshimoto

"No road is long with good company"
— Turkish Proverb

"True love is rare, and it's the only thing that gives life real meaning."
— Nicholas Sparks, Message in a Bottle

"Don't it always seem to go, that you don't know what you've got till it's gone." — Joni Mitchell

"You don't take away my choices. You are my choice." — Colleen Houck

"Every woman deserves a man to ruin her lipstick, not her mascara" — Charlotte Tilbury

"Life began after I fell in love with you"
— Brad Hodge

"The heart has a heart of its own." — Morrissey

"Love is a smoke made with the fume of sighs."
— William Shakespeare, Romeo and Juliet

Quotes to Couple By

"If I had a flower for every time I thought of you...I could walk through my garden forever."
— Alfred Lord Tennyson

"Love is the answer, and you know that for sure; Love is a flower, you've got to let it grow."
— John Lennon

"Life is a journey, not a destination; there are no mistakes, just chances we've taken."
— India.Arie

"I really don't know what "I love you" means. I think it means "Don't leave me here alone."
— Neil Gaiman

"How do you spell 'love'?" - Piglet
"You don't spell it...you feel it." - Pooh"
— A.A. Milne

"Storms make trees take deeper roots."
— Dolly Parton

"Love is just a word until someone comes along and gives it meaning." — Paulo Coelho

"Lovers don't finally meet somewhere. They're in each other all along." — Rumi

A Letter to Each Other On Our Anniversary

A Letter to Each Other On Our Anniversary

A Letter to You On Your Birthday

A Letter to You On Your Birthday

NOTES

NOTES

NOTES

NOTES

NOTES

NOTES

NOTES

NOTES

NOTES

NOTES

NOTES

NOTES

NOTES

NOTES

NOTES

NOTES

NOTES

NOTES

NOTES

NOTES

NOTES

NOTES

NOTES

NOTES

NOTES

NOTES

NOTES

NOTES

NOTES

NOTES

NOTES

NOTES

NOTES

NOTES

NOTES

NOTES

NOTES

NOTES

NOTES

NOTES

NOTES

NOTES

NOTES

NOTES

Did You Like This Workbook?

Thank you for taking the time to use this workbook. It's a huge deal for me and I couldn't be more grateful. If you found what I have created to be helpful, please take a quick moment and write a review on Amazon. Your thoughts and your comments help me get better at this thing I love.

It would also be great if you could pass my workbooks along to friends and family. Thank you and please have a wonderful rest of your day.

About Jeffrey Mason

Jeffrey Mason has spent twenty plus years leading teams and projects and helping organizations meet their objectives and employees realize their goals. He loves mentoring and helping people move forward both professionally and personally. He is a dad, a certified coach, an author, and a pretty good cook. He is committed to reminding everyone that being human is hard and the more we do for each other, the more we do for ourselves.

Feel free to send him an email at hello@jeffreymason.com. He would love to hear from you.